Real Estate Investing For Beginners:

How to Make Money in Real Estate Market

By

Robert Alderman

ISBN-13: 978-1503274082

Table of Contents

Introduction 5

Chapter 1. What is real Estate and Real Estate Investing? 7

Chapter 2. Types of Real Estate Investments 9

Chapter 3. Real Estate Investing Process 15

Chapter 4. The 4 Best Way To Make Money By Real Estate Investing 22

Chapter 5. Blue print Strategy for Real Estate Business 25

Chapter 6. Why to Invest Your Money in Real Estate? 27

Final Words 30

Thank You Page 31

Real Estate Investing For Beginners: How to Make Money in Real Estate Market

By Robert Alderman

© Copyright 2014 Robert Alderman

Reproduction or translation of any part of this work beyond that permitted by section 107 or 108 of the 1976 United States Copyright Act without permission of the copyright owner is unlawful. Requests for permission or further information should be addressed to the author.

This publication is designed to provide accurate and authoritative information in regard to the subject matter covered. This work is sold with the understanding that the publisher is not engaged in rendering legal, accounting, or other professional services. If legal advice or other expert assistance is required, the services of a competent professional person should be sought.

First Published, 2014

Printed in the United States of America

Introduction

The most difficult thing in life is to make decision about investments. People most commonly encounter a lot of queries and do not find any way to get the right answers like how to invest my money to make more profit? Which business is best to invest in? How much investment do I need initially? And the list of questions goes on. But unfortunately, finding the right guidance is the hardest thing. This step by step guide is intended to educate you and answer your all queries related to the top business opportunity having a lot of fame from past 50 years and in the future too, i.e. Real Estate Investing.

Real estate investment has got its place in the top business categories. Accordingly to different researches and surveys, in last decades the people interest in investing in real estate had tremendously increased. This trend is not only specific to males, but females have also shown interest in starting and establishing real estate businesses. The buying and selling of the property earn you huge profit as compared to any other business. Mostly, there is no loss in the real estate business, in fact with passing time the value of property get raised.

Investing in real estate is not just finding the new place to live in, but also enjoying the profit when you sell after sometime. The real estate market has grown tremendously and earned people big profits in little time. If you have little money and you want to start a business which really won't earn you loss then, it is best to start your business with the small amount of money in real estate and gradually extend it by earning profit. Discover the strategies, secrets and advantages of taking start in the world of real estate and establish your own billion dollars business.

Chapter 1. What is real Estate and Real Estate Investing?

Real estate is refers to the property and anything attached to it like building build over it, shopping malls and even agriculture land. Most commonly the real estate if used for the residential property, but it is not limited to only land having house build over it. Real estate involves the property and land both in the rural or urban area, however the value of the property is determined by the location.

The real estate investments works quite simply, as you invest your money in buying the property from the other party or the owner of the property and sell the same property on profit to any other group of investors. The money involve keep on rolling by making profit. Real Estate involves different types of property and you can become the investor of some specific category or even choose to become the all-rounder, it all depends on your own capability and management skills. It also matter, whether you looking for part time business or a full time.

The time is crucial in running any business, your income directly depends on the time you invest in your business. If you really want to take your business to the new levels, then it is best to nurture it with your full time attention and care. You can't make huge profit without investing less effort, so start little but start wisely.

Chapter 2. Types of Real Estate Investments

As mentioned above the real estate is quite a broader field for investment and it involves different types of properties and dealing in one kind of property is quite different than other in all aspects. Commonly, the real estate is divided into 6 categories as follows:

1. Residential Real Estate Investments

Residential real estate investments involve the selling and buying of the residential properties like home, flats etc. It usually involves the rent services too. People rent the residential property for some months or years and earn the profit through rents paid by the customers each month. The rent duration and amount is agreeable between the customer and the client and most of the time both the parties sign a rental or lease agreement to avoid any complications in the future.

2. Industrial Real Estate Investments

Industrial real estate investments involves the property under the use of industries whether it's small or large. The storage houses, car wash and many other business comes under the same category are known as industrial property. This type of the property is also rent for some time and for specific purpose. The rent of the property get increased each year, as the price of the property goes up. Hence, by renting to the same customer you can increase the profit earn each year.

In Industrial real estate investments, the customers can rent the equipment and devices too, which they can utilize and have to pay some rent of the equipment involve each month. Like in car wash, all the equipment and devices involved in the car washing can be acquired on rent. The ROI of this type of real estate services is quite high and this is also a most prefer type of investment when comes to investing large amount of money in real estate.

3. Commercial Real Estate Investments

The commercial real estate investments involve renting the property to businesses and companies to utilize for offices. If you have some good money and the land, you can easily construct spacious offices and lease your property to small companies, startups and business to setup up their offices. These type of rental services are quite beneficial, as every year the rent get increased to some percent, accordingly to the change in the value of the property or currently observed rental prices in the market. So, it simply means the profit you earn on your property get raised by passing each year, without spending much on renovation and other expenditure.

It is your choice to provide the office furnished or unfurnished. Mostly, the startup companies preferred the furnished offices, as they can't do it on their own due to financial limitations. A good amount of rent can be earned each month. This type of investments also involves the rental agreement between both the client and customer to legalize the whole process and to avoid any trouble in the future.

4. Retail Real Estate Investments

Retail real estate investments consists of the property comes under the shopping malls, shopping stores as well as retail stores. It also works as the same way the above mentioned investments do. The customer can rent the shops to utilize and customize as per their requirements and each month pay the fixed amount of rent to the property holder.

Sometimes, the property holder also fixed some percentage of amount from the store earning as the fee for the renovation and other expenditure of the building. It also involves the rental agreement between both the parties involved. The customer has the responsibility to keep the property in the good condition by continuous renovation as required.

5. Mixed Real Estate Investments

Mixed real estate investments involved, when the people invest in more than one category of the real estate investment and earn huge return on profit. The common practice for beginners and starters in the real estate business is to initially stick to one category and when their business get established, they would have started to earn good profit, they can easily start investing in other categories too.

The commercial and industrial investments mostly comes under the same category and people invest their money in both at the same time. However, the commercial investments are good for those people having huge amount to invest. If you want to start with little amount and do not like to take big risk then it's better to start with the residential real estate investments.

6. Real Estate Investments Trusts

Real Estate Investments Trusts work like the stock, where you spend money to buy the shares in the property and earn money on it according to Return on Investment acquired each month. There are many groups working on these type on investments.

There are no direct mortgage, closing costs and contract involved. There are different types of Real estate investment trusts, each specialize in specific category like in residential, commercial, etc. It is best business investment for the mediocre investors, as you can earn an easy profit without going through any hassle of property acquisition.

Before stepping in the business of real estate, it is necessary that you understand all the above mentioned categories and choose wisely accordingly to the money in hand and amount of risk you can take. Not any single business is risk free, but it all depends on how wisely you make quick decision on investment and which strategies you utilize to compensate any loss. The little knowledge of your selected industry can also earn you a huge loss. It is always better to conduct your own research on the location, you are going to invest your money.

Chapter 3. Real Estate Investing Process

The real estate investments involve the money invest in buying, renting and selling of the property. The real estate investing refers to the ownership, sell, buy, management and purchase of the property for the profit. Although, nowadays the real estate businesses are everywhere, even then the market demand for the initiation of new real estate businesses are still there, as it has outperformed the other business due to high demand equally from the side of both the clients and the customers.

Currently, as the world is turning into the global village, the boundaries or real estate investing has also extended and people has started to their own international real estate firms and companies to facilitate opening of companies branches in different countries as well opening of shopping outlets of the same brand in different countries. This new market trend has created a lot of space for the new investor, both on small and large level to invest their money in the real estate.

Follow these steps to start a Business in Real estate Investing:

Step 1: Do the research

Whenever, you intend to start new business, it is always recommended to do the research and market analysis on your own. Look for the latest trends, investments opportunities. Learn the effective strategies. Get yourself acquaint with the business terminologies and look for the success businesses out there.

Study their success stories, know their strategies and get inspiration. Sit with the people having knowledge of the market, get tips and not down everything for record. Look for the groups or companies involved in the business in the area, you are looking to start business in.

Step 2: Choose the Niche

After you are done with the research part and now well equipped with the market knowledge and different niche. The next step is to choose the niche for your business. Choose the one which of your investment, meet your requirements, suits your pocket and easy to manage. Moreover, it also best to get success in the area of the business and location.

The most common type of niche involved in the real estate investment are the commercial, rental, industrial, foreclosure and retail property. Choose wisely because the fate of your business depends on the niche you choose to invest your money.

Step 3: Get the advice of the attorney

All the real estate business involved an important aspect of law. Without considering its important you can't keep yourself out of legal charges and crimes. It is best whenever you setup any business, do get a professional advice or law person to avoid any legal trouble in the future.

It is equally true for the real estate business, in fact the whole real estate is based upon legal processes, agreements, legal and rental contracts. Therefore, consult any attorney specialized in real estate issues. Learn about the taxes involve and how to legalize your business and register it with the government.

Only an attorney can help you to prepare the agreement and contract papers, can suggest you best law practices to lower down the government taxes on the properties especially on the commercial as well as industrial properties buying and selling. He can help you understand your rights and requirements. Provide your business full protection from the fraudulent and scams customers.

Step 4: Know your competitors

When you searched the market, you come to know about your competitors well. Ignoring your competitors is not the wise thing, you can't succeed in the business where you can't out performed your competitors by providing your customers better services.

Do not take your competitors easy, always strive to renew and add good practices in the product and services you are providing. Otherwise you will left behind in the market by your competitors. In beginnings, it is always difficult to make your place in the market without applying effective strategies of the success in any business, which you will learn shortly.

Step 5: Must have enough money

For setting up any business, you must have enough money in hand to get a high return on investment. Otherwise, your business will shut down in some months and you get depressed and leave it yourself. If you got any good opportunity and short fall in money. The best thing is to lend it from any source like from friend, other property businesses and even you can lend it from the banks.

Lending money from the bank also involved the interest and taxes. Carefully lend the money without any hassle and blind decisions. Sometimes the step taken in rush cause your business a huge loss, which you are not realizing at the time of acquiring money. Some companies also offer new startups with low and even zero interest rate lending services. So, everything demands good research of the market, so keep on doing research and never cease it even if you become the top business of the industry.

Step 6: Approach the Real Estate Agent

If you are facing difficulty finding the right customers or potential people to lend or rent your property, then the best option is to approach any real estate agent. Because these agents have the good record of the customers and clients and even find you the one.

The real estate agents do not offer their services for free, they charge specific percentage of fee on per successful deal. So, find the right real estate agent, who is not only authentic but also the offering the beat service sin the lowest amount of fee. You can even keep these agents as your business shareholders. This way you can extend your business reach to the root level without providing any resources to the agents but just some fixed amount of money on every successful deal.

Step 7: Get the qualified and dedicated staff

Each and every business requires some HR personnel to efficiently manage the whole business, to keep the things in order and on record. You can't establish a successful business on your own. After you are done with the above mentioned steps. The final thing you need is to get the efficient and dedicated HR for running your business successfully.

Build the team of young, energetic and knowledgeable people to conduct transactions, deals, research, and office work as well as to manage the outreach responsibilities. Divide your business into different sections and hire the people accordingly. You can keep people on monthly salary and even on shares. Talk about it with your law attorney and get his best advice on hiring the real estate staff.

Not all the staff you require must have the knowledge of the real estate, some may require the knowledge of computers for office work and record keeping. Some must have good communication and marketing skills to extend the reach of your business and gain more customer. The experience and knowledge required will depend on the type of work involved.

Following the above mentioned steps, you can easily start your new business in the real estate investing and can run it successfully without facing any trouble and issue.

Chapter 4. The 4 Best Way To Make Money By Real Estate Investing

You can make many using various ways in the real estate business, but these 4 methods are quite effective to run a successful business and to earn a good capital on your investments:

1. Investing money in the land have the potential of turning into future big shopping malls and commercial areas. The land around your property turn into a busier place and people starting to visit the place frequently like shopping and retail stores. If the area turned into the commercial market or the land around your property developed into commercial property. The value of your property will automatically goes up. Sometimes the area is abandon and does not have much progress but in coming years, the land has the potential of turning into busier place. This type of land is quite profitable and can earn you big cash in just some years.

2. The second strategy is to establish the cash flow by renting your property for some time. The property will remain in use and you will earn the cash every month. The rent goes up as the market prices raises and this way your profit will also increase on changing sin market values. If your property is surrounded by the commercial area, then the rent will be high and you will earn more profit. Cash flow income can also be generated by the industrial and commercially rent property and equipment. Even if you are not selling your property, you will keep making money from rent and you can sell your property anytime you want. This is the best way to make continuous profit instead of abandoning your property empty and only earning profit on selling it.

3. Earn money by getting into management of real estate affairs for big companies like become the real estate agent and earn profit on every sell and buying. By helping companies finding the potential customers you can earn a good profit out of their income. Mostly, the companies hire the personnel to handle their real estate matters and outreach the potential buyers. Mostly brokers and real estate agents are the ones people contact to sell and buy the property. As they can access even the common man, but companies can't go at every location and motivate people. So they hire the agents having knowledge of the people and location, hence the big companies utilize their services for establishing and as well as extending their real estate business.

4. The last method to earn money in real estate business is through ancillary real estate investments. Like providing or supplying the equipment to the offices, offering the machines for laundry to the offices or people of the specific area. Supply machinery to the car washers and earn the rent of the machinery each month. Providing the furnished apartments on rent and charge the maintenance of the apartment and furniture. By this strategy, a lot of profit can be earned in the real estate business.

Chapter 5. Blue print Strategy for Real Estate Business

When you start any business, it is important to clearly define your vision or goals and keep record of them in the form a map, so that you keep consulting it during your journey and keep reminding yourself of your goals. This is the best practice for a business success which is priceless and motivating to always look forward and work hard.

1. First thing you can do is to define your goal. Then divide your goal into simple and achievable steps. Like you set a goal to achieve some profit in one year. Now divide the goal that every month you will earn that much profit to reach your goal.

2. Now second this is to draw a road map of your goal and its final destination. It's like defining a journey or story. It is a pretty interesting work and involves creativity too. Clearly mention your goal, time period it requires as well as the picture of final result.

3. No the execution comes into action, You know your goal well and now you need to execute the things to reach the goal by start implementing the things you have planned for the goal achievement.

4. Once we have started to work on our goal, now it's the time to apply the strategies to raise the bar of the profit. It is important to turn our goals or dreams into reality. Work each day on applying and analyze the strategies and keep the one which really works for you.

5. At the end keep working towards you goal and see it in action by acquiring the profit to set for the particular goal. Repeat the same blue print strategy for your each and every real estate business goal and reach the new avenues of success by fulfilling your dreams.

Chapter 6. Why to Invest Your Money in Real Estate?

Every business has some perks of investment in them and real estate investing too has some benefits for the investors and especially for those people who are looking for some long term profits.

1. The best thing in the real estate is the capital earn each month after compensating the real expenditures. It also goes up as the market value raises and hence your profit ultimately raises without doing anything.

2. Secondly, as the land turns into a more busier place the property values goes up, it will also earn your more cash whether you sell the property and keep it on rent, both ways your capital will keep on increasing.

3. You can attain double benefit, unlike other business, you do not have to wait without gaining profit. If you rent your property, you keep on earning some profit each month and as the price of the property goes up, sell it and earn more profit. So your property will earn you constant profit sometimes low and sometimes quite high.

4. Real estate business is the best retirement plan. Buy a property and rent it to the customer. Earn the cash each month and keep it as your savings. If you are a terrible saver even then you do not need to be worried about, unless and until you really lose your land or property. If you have a property at a good location, then it is the best saving for your retirement life. So all terrible savers out there, finally you have something good to invest in to have a peaceful life after retirement.

5. Its tax free, during cash flow you do not need to pay any tax. You buy something and sell it by earning profit over it without paying any taxes.

6. By real estate investing you can secure the future of yourself and your family. In this world where death can come at any time. You can leave a good amount of money for your children in the form of property. Do not forget, by passing time the value of property get increased and your family can get more profit and benefit by wisely utilizing it.

7. This is the best business where you can start with little money and by the time extend by utilizing profit earned over it without any loss and risk. This could only be possible if you follow the proper legal process to avoid fraudulent and scams.

Final Words

Although real estate investing is one of the most progressive business, however it is necessary to take care of legal issues involved otherwise you can lose your whole property and can't even claim it back. Make sure to not execute any property transfer without involving any attorney in the process to authenticate the people and property involved.

Real estate investing not only the best business for the starters but also a life time guaranteed savings for the family or retired persons. Your money remain save in the form or property and even you can earn profit on it. The property price is also keep on increasing and you can sell it at any time. So, start your research today and establish a successful business in real estate investing and secure the future of your family.

Thank You Page

I want to personally thank you for reading my book. I hope you found information in this book useful and I would be very grateful if you could leave your honest review about this book. I certainly want to thank you in advance for doing this.

www.ingramcontent.com/pod-product-compliance
Lightning Source LLC
Chambersburg PA
CBHW070732180526
45167CB00004B/1723